AD[illegible]Ú

Great Daughter

THE STRUGGLES AND VICTORIES OF A WORKING WOMAN

PAMELA NGOZI ABAH

Author services by Opulent Books
www.OpulentBooks.net

ISBN: 978-1-916691-45-2

All scripture quotations are taken from KING JAMES VERSION (KJV): KING JAMES VERSION, *public domain.*

"

Dedication

To God, for guiding my path, showing me the way, and providing endless inspiration. May this work bring glory to Your name.

"

Table of Contents

Acknowledgements

I want to give special mention to my husband, Edward Abah, who is a strong pillar of support–very caring, understanding, and my greatest motivation. To my parents, Mr Peter Obiekwu and Mrs Patricia Obiekwu, whose prayers and support have brought me this far. Their commitment to my education ensured I received the best; I am an author today because of their dedication. To my amazing siblings, Chuks, Shirley, Uche, and Chiedu, I can't thank you enough for being there for me. To my in-laws, the Abahs, thank you.

Finally, to my spiritual parents and their families–Prof and Dcns Tobih, Pst and Dcns Soyinka, Prophet and Mummy Prof Iyunade, Pst and Dcns Toba Ojo, Dcns Adeboye, Pst and Dcns Izuidu, Pst Ebojoh and the Epochis–thank you so much for your prayers and encouragement. I also want to acknowledge the Ogundirans, Emma, Mr and Mrs Okonji, I say a big thank you. To Prof C. Nwabueze. Thank you for giving me the extra push to get this done. To the CGMI Anwai and PSBM family, I love you. To my dear friends that are too many to mention–thank you so much for your love.

Introduction

The title "ADA ÚKWÚ," meaning "Great Daughter," is a name my mother fondly calls me when I have done something beyond her expectations. It came as a surprise when it was given to me in a dream as the title of my book, and it holds a special place in my heart. This book, inspired by this profound title, aims to encourage and uplift daughters everywhere—whether they are married, aspiring to marry, navigating the journey of pregnancy, or encountering delays and difficulties in life.

"ADA ÚKWÚ" tells the story of a daughter who, despite the challenges, inspires other daughters, Christian sisters, and working women to persevere. It is evidence of the strength of women who juggle careers and motherhood, face setbacks, and yet remain steadfast in their faith that God's timing is perfect. This book reassures readers that, despite the hardships, God will make everything beautiful in His time.

I hope readers will find inspiration in these pages, especially working mothers, newly married women, those hoping to get married, and those believing in God for the fruit of the womb. This book is dedicated to women who have endured the pain of losing a pregnancy or waiting for years for a child, encouraging them to never lose hope and to continue being a great daughter, wife, and member of society.

My personal journey has not been without its trials. As a committed Christian, I have faced moments of discouragement and heartbreak. Yet, through God's grace and the support of my loving spouse, family and friends, I have learned to pick up the pieces and keep moving forward. This book also underscores the importance of waiting for the right partner and surrounding oneself with positive, faith-filled individuals.

Significant moments in my life, such as experiencing an ectopic pregnancy, undergoing surgery, and enduring career setbacks, have shaped who I am today. Despite these trials, I have remained hopeful and resilient, knowing that my story is still unfolding and will culminate in a testimony of God's faithfulness.

I am sharing my story to inspire other women to keep believing and hoping, even after experiencing profound losses. I want to remind them to stay connected with positive influences, engage in activities that bring joy, and continue to trust in God's plan.

Through the themes of working motherhood, faith, resilience, and the power of supportive relationships, "ADA ÚKWÚ" explores the depths of pain and the heights of hope. Readers will find scriptures, practical advice on navigating challenges, and encouragement to keep giving and believing, regardless of their circumstances.

The impact I hope to achieve is to inspire readers to pick up the pieces, stand strong, and continue to believe in themselves and God's promises. "ADA ÚKWÚ" is a call to action for women to keep striving, giving, and hoping, knowing that God will ultimately bless them with the desires of their hearts.

Chapter 1

Work Life

"You're pregnant, says the gynaecologist. I felt so delighted and over the moon. It was about five months after my wedding to my university sweetheart, Edward. I got back home to my uncle Austin's house, where I was residing after I got my banking job. I told myself that I needed the perfect opportunity to reveal this good news to my uncle's dear wife, Aunty Awele.

I decided to go ahead and tell my husband the good news. I called Edward, and we shared the news. He was so excited and happy that he was soon going to be a father. We laughed over the phone, recalling beautiful moments from our colourful wedding, a practice we're used to. It was like our daily breakfast routine that kept us together despite the distance my job had brought. I was a professional banker at one of the notable banks in Nigeria. I worked as a marketer, tasked with bringing in new clients, maintaining existing relationships, and offering services to enhance daily business operations.

The next day at work, I moved with caution to avoid any disruptions. I didn't want my high-heeled shoes to cause havoc to my system. I was walking as if on eggshells and laughed at myself because I was used to walking really fast, so it was something I had to get used to. I performed my duties with joy, met with clients, and concluded my day by rushing off to catch a bus before the typical Lagos traffic built up. That's one thing you can't take away from Lagos—heavy traffic!

The next day, I resumed early and checked the office portal and noticed that my profile was still showing my maiden name. I didn't remind the human resources department because I had already sent the required documents for the name change, including the wedding certificate, newspaper publication, and court affidavit. These are required to change your name after marriage. I decided to send a reminder because this was taking months, and I couldn't wait to officially be addressed as Mrs Abah in the office.

I also sent another email indicating my interest in getting a transfer to any of our branches in Asaba, Delta State, where my husband resided. I had to get these sorted really fast so I could be with my husband before I got really heavy and would be unable to relocate. I drifted into thoughts, imagining how I would decorate my unborn baby's room. I came back to reality when my friend called out to me. She said the business development manager, known as the BDM, wanted a short meeting with all the marketers.

I cleared my desk and headed to the meeting room. We were welcomed with the usual threats:

"If you don't bring in big accounts, consider yourselves out." Our performance as a branch had improved, but a lot of work still needed to be done, especially by most of the marketers. We took turns mentioning our deals in the pipeline, which covered clients we hoped to meet, clients we had met and held conversations with, prospects, and ideas to bring in more clients. The life of a marketer in the banking industry is filled with uncertainties, and you can be asked to leave if you aren't meeting your targets. These meetings were a nightmare, especially if you had no clients or prospects to present.

We hit the road again as usual. I headed to a prospect who is an oil and gas dealer. This client specialised in the downstream segment, which deals with refining and marketing, and so it was a big catch for me. He was doing quite well for himself, and I got to offer him the various packages we have for clients in that line of business. He listened to me keenly and agreed to start doing business with us as he was looking to have more branches outside Lagos. I was so excited because everything seemed to be working out for my good. I gave him the account forms and showed him the sections to fill out and those to ignore. We agreed on a day for me to come back to pick up the completed forms. Happy and fulfilled, I got on the road with Abdullahi, who was the office driver assigned to marketers.

We had a very good bond. I have a great relationship with drivers, cleaners, and security officials. It was a conscious thing for me to ensure I showed love and care to this cadre of staff. I made sure I was good to these people because I could feel their pain. I was intentional in dealing with this group of staff, going out of my way to be exceptionally good to them because I felt they did a lot with little recognition.

Abdullahi and I always enjoyed each other's company. Driving time was a moment for him to discuss his eldest son's progress in his studies with me. I never failed to listen with keen interest and offer advice, sometimes topping it off with a little act of kindness. We chatted, and I told him it was a happy day for me since I finally secured a deal with the oil tycoon.

I got to the office quite late because we were held up by the congested Lagos traffic that was already building up. I completed my call memo, which is what you do as a marketer every day after your marketing activities; you note down who you visited, the clients you saw, and a brief summary of what you discussed. It's something you must do to show what you've accomplished for the day. This time, I was happy because I had something tangible to present to my BDM the next morning. My friend Dorothy checked on me to see if I was ready to go home.

We would either go home together, or I go home with my cousin, Ruth. I was ready, and we left together, heading back to my uncle's house where I lived. My uncle and his lovely wife were in the sitting room. I greeted them with a smile and then went to my room. I shared the same room with my cousins Isioma and Daisy, and it was always fun because we had a lot to talk about. Isioma was home, and I told her about my pregnancy. She was really happy for me. I told her I would inform my uncle and his family when I got a good opportunity to do so.

I really wanted to speak to my aunt privately to break the news to her first, and then have her share it with the rest of the family. Isioma went on and on telling me to be careful at work and ensure I don't get stressed. "Get flat shoes," she said because I didn't like flat shoes and wore heels daily. She encouraged me to give her money to get one pair of flat shoes, which I did.

How can you not get stressed when, on some days, the office vehicle is not available and you have to do long walks and jump on buses? The unfortunate seats in the buses, the bad roads, and the hectic traffic all put together create a super stressful day, topped off with the daily anxiety of not meeting targets. "Nawa!"—this is an exclamation in the popular Pidgin language we speak in Nigeria, used to express the complexity and exhaustion of a situation.

Thank God it's Friday! We had our usual meeting, and in turns, we shared our previous day's achievements and what we intended to accomplish over the weekend. I excitedly talked about my oil and gas client and the progress I made in getting the forms, still waiting for the client to submit more documentation. The response from my boss was for me to do more to ensure big money was deposited into the account. It was not the reaction I had expected. Well, he is the boss and entitled to the way he runs the shop.

I took it in good faith and hoped for the meeting to be over. I drifted into thoughts, asking myself when I would leave Lagos to meet my sweetheart in Asaba.

Fridays were usually my travelling days to Delta State, but I could no longer embark on such trips because I was pregnant and didn't want the stress.

The weekend came, and my good colleague Olumide promised to take me to a beach. I love going to the beach; it has a way of calming my nerves. He picked me up, and we went to one of the popular beaches in Lagos, Bar Beach. We got fish and drinks and talked about work, life, and how it feels to be married.

I want to take this opportunity to encourage working women everywhere. Whatever job you find yourself doing, strive to perform it to the best of your ability. This is a principle I have lived by: to be diligent and to always give my best effort.

Often, you may find yourself in less-than-ideal situations at work. However, it is essential to remember that it is your attitude that truly matters. Your best is always ahead of you, but it starts with what you can achieve in your current place and position. As it is written in Ecclesiastes 9:10, "Whatever your hand finds to do, do it with all your might." Furthermore, approach your work as if you are doing it for the Lord, giving it your utmost dedication and sincerity.

By maintaining a positive and proactive attitude, and by consistently putting forth your best effort, you can overcome challenges and excel in any role you undertake.

After about two hours, I got home, and my uncle's wife was busy baking in the kitchen with Isioma helping her. Aunty Awele baked very nice cakes, and my favourite was her sponge cake. She was such a sweet person. I was excited because she always kept some extra cake for the house whenever she baked.

Days passed, and I still didn't have the opportunity to tell my uncle's wife about my pregnancy because I got home quite late, and either she was in her bedroom asleep, super busy baking, or watching television with my uncle.

Sundays are our worship days; we all went to church. As usual, the sermons were great, and the choir did an amazing job. The church was full as schools were still on Easter holiday, so teenagers were everywhere. After the service, we all moved into my uncle's car. Getting home, it was food time, and I got my portion of rice and stew, which was the usual Sunday meal, and it was really delicious. My usual routine after eating my Sunday meal is to sort out my weekly outfits, do some ironing, and then have a good siesta.

A call from my sweetheart woke me up, and we talked about how I was feeling. Edward is so caring, as he has always been, even in the days of our dating.

"I'm doing well," I responded.

We chatted and laughed, discussed the church service, and he was particularly concerned about the pressure I was under at work.

"I can't quit now, dear," I said to him.

"A lot of women still do this work and have lots of kids. I have colleagues who have three, four kids."

He replied, "I'm not asking you to quit. I just wish I could help you with work so you won't be under any form of pressure. I can't wait for you to move to Asaba."

"I totally understand, my husband," I said. He has always cared deeply for me and would do all he can to ensure I'm not stressed.

"I wish you had been granted this transfer so I could be with you every day," he said.

"Very soon, when there is a vacancy for me in Asaba, I will then be with you," I assured him. "We have to keep hoping and praying." Our lengthy call lasted as usual, professing our love for each other and discussing our plans for the future. We said goodbye, looking forward to the next conversation.

After I broke the news of my pregnancy to my husband, I also told my parents. They were absolutely supportive, loving, and caring. I recall calling my mum, and she was over the moon. She had hoped and prayed for me to have my own children as well, especially since my younger sister was already married and had a daughter at that time. She was hoping and praying that I could also be blessed with children early.

She was very happy that this had come to reality. She gave all the advice she could— you know, the typical African mum, listing all the foods and things she expected me to stay away from. I said, "Yes, Mum. Yes, Mum, I got all of that." She was very excited and said a big prayer for me. My dad was also in the background, hoping and praying that this pregnancy journey would be beautiful. They were very, very excited, and I was just happy for them as well.

It is important to pay close attention to the people who celebrate your successes and achievements. These individuals show their genuine support and happiness for you, which is evidence of their positive influence on your life. Their joy in your victories reflects their true friendship and loyalty.

Equally significant is noticing those who do not share in your happiness when you have good news to share. Their lack of enthusiasm or even indifference can reveal a great deal about their character and their feelings towards you. This observation can be quite telling, as it highlights those who may not have your best interests at heart.

In my own experience, my family has always rejoiced in my successes, providing a solid support system that I am deeply grateful for. It is crucial to recognise that not everyone will respond positively to your achievements. Therefore, it is wise to be discerning about with whom you share your good news. Protect your positive energy and joy by confiding in those who truly care for you and will celebrate your accomplishments sincerely.

Understanding and recognising these dynamics can help you build stronger, more supportive relationships and avoid potential negativity from those who may not have your best interests in mind.

> *"Your most important work is always ahead of you and never behind you."*
>
> **— Stephen Covey**

Chapter 2

Broken

The sun was already blazing in the sky, casting a golden hue over the bustling streets of Lagos. The city was alive with the sounds of honking cars, street vendors calling out their wares, and the rhythmic clatter of footsteps on the pavement. As I stepped into the office early, as was my routine, the air was filled with a sense of purpose and anticipation. After a moment of quiet reflection and my morning prayers, I joined my colleagues for the general morning prayers.

My plan was to visit small business owners in the

typical hustle and bustle of Lagos market, specifically Balogun Market. I intended to discuss small loans for small businesses. Balogun is a very large market filled with retailers of all sorts. You'll find many young businessmen and women who import accessories, jewellery, shoes, fabrics, and bags. Business is quite lucrative because many people come from various places to buy items from Balogun Market. The shoe and bag section are always very busy, as people come from different parts of the country to buy in large quantities. I decided to go out with my colleague Loretta, who is very familiar with this area of the market. This was a typical no-car day—there are days when we don't have access to the branch vehicles.

So, we put on our flat shoes and headed to the market, which is not far from my office. I prayed earnestly that I could secure one or two businesses because I hadn't acquired any clients recently apart from the oil mogul, and there was a lot of pressure on me. Accompanied by my colleague Loretta, we hit the road and entered the market. We managed to connect with a few young men who import bags and shoes and made some good contacts. Fortunately for both Loretta and myself, we found two clients willing to open accounts with us and explore our loan options.

The way the loan process works is that you have to open an account with us first and maintain a banking relationship for at least three to six months before we can consider processing a loan, depending on the turnover of your account. We helped these young men fill out the account opening forms and assisted them throughout the process, spending practically the whole day in their shops. We were also able to buy some very affordable bags for ourselves. Normally, these sellers allow only bulk buying of women's bags in dozens, but we managed to buy one each at the wholesale price because we had established a relationship with them. It was also a sign that we are committed to the success of their business and not just after giving the loans. Their success is also our success. It was a very fruitful day.

We returned to the office feeling very happy.

Loretta had to leave early because she lives quite far from the office. I stayed back to complete my call memo and make sure everything was in order for the next morning. We were going to have our usual meeting to discuss what we had achieved the previous day and the deals we had in the pipeline. It was one of those days when I was really happy because I had something tangible to discuss the next morning.

Most of my colleagues had already started packing up and leaving. Dorothy, my friend, also left, and the colleague who sometimes takes me home had gone too. I was still working on my call notes when my cousin Ruth called to ask if I was done for the day. I told her I had almost concluded my call memo, and she asked why I was still in the office and mentioned that she was already at our head office, which is not very far from my branch. She decided to wait for me at a junction close to the office. She called to let me know she was there, so we could go home together.

I tidied up what I was doing and shut down my

workstation. I decided to use the restroom before calling security to lock up the office. So, I went into the ladies' to ease myself. As I was about to get up, I couldn't move. There was this excruciating pain like I had never experienced before. I tried everything I could to stand up, but I couldn't.

My phone started ringing again. I had left my bag by the door to the entrance of the ladies', so I didn't have it with me. I knew I had to get to my phone. I managed to get off the toilet seat and crawled to my phone. When I picked it up, it was my cousin Ruth, asking what I was still doing in the office. I told her I was in pain and couldn't get up. She was shocked because we had spoken only about ten minutes earlier. She told me she was rushing to the office to help.

Ruth managed to get to the office, and with the help of the security guard, she came in through the back door. I was still on the floor, in severe pain. She and the security guard managed to help me out of the office. My office is on the first floor, so they carefully took me down the stairs.

We managed to get to the ground floor and waited for a taxi. While we were there, I was still in pain, and passers-by were watching and wondering what was going on. I couldn't explain what was happening to me. Many thoughts crept into my head. I hoped I wasn't losing my baby. That was the first thing that came to mind. Could it be period pain? But why would I have a period when I'm pregnant? So many things crossed my mind—could it be something I ate? Is it food poisoning? So many thoughts were crowding my head. Ruth managed to get a cab for us, and we headed straight home.

While we were in the cab, I couldn't sit upright, so I lay on Ruth's lap. It was a long journey home because of the crazy Lagos traffic. The taxi driver managed to get us home in about 45 minutes. When we got home, I went inside. As I mentioned earlier, I live with my uncle, his wife, and children, along with my cousin Isioma. My uncle and his wife were in the sitting room and asked what was going on. Ruth explained the situation to them. He insisted I must go to the hospital, but I wanted to rest and thought I would feel better by the next morning. I just wanted to take some rest. I told him that if I slept, I believed I would be fine by morning.

My uncle, who is very health-conscious and doesn't take such matters lightly, wasn't having it. I must point out here that I am grateful I was staying with my uncle. If I hadn't been, I would have gone to bed with that pain because that's typical of me, and I can't imagine what might have happened. The hospital is usually my last resort; I usually try to find a home remedy first.

The pain was getting so bad that I couldn't get up from the sofa in the living room. My uncle's son, Dumebi, who is young but very strong, was able to lift me up and carry me like a baby. For that, I am very grateful to him.

My uncle's wife grabbed her wallet, and my cousin Dumebi drove me to the closest hospital, accompanied by Ruth. It happened to be the same hospital where I had gone for the pregnancy test a few weeks ago. It was that hospital that had confirmed I was pregnant. When we arrived, the doctor recognised me and said, "Oh, aren't you the one who came in some days ago? I told you that you were pregnant, right?" I said yes. He responded, "Oh no, what is going on?"

This was how my aunt found out I was pregnant. I had been looking for an opportunity to tell her, but I hadn't been able to. Either she was already in bed when I returned home, or she was talking to her husband, or there was something else preventing me from telling her about the pregnancy.

Thanks to the doctor's experience, I was taken to a room in the hospital. He asked me how I was feeling, and I described the pain. He said, "I hope it's not what I'm thinking." When he said that, I started going in and out of consciousness. Sometimes I could hear, and then everything would go silent again.

I knew the doctor took a syringe and injected it into the right side of my stomach, but no blood came out. He tried the left side, and there was blood. He said, "She's bleeding internally; she needs surgery immediately. I don't have the facilities to handle this kind of surgery."

"But I think I know what is going on," the doctor said. He provided a brief summary of his diagnosis for me to present at the next hospital. My cousin Dumebi, along with Ruth and my aunt Awele, helped me back to the car. Unfortunately, the hospital didn't have an ambulance to convey me, but Dumebi was confident he could find the hospital. It was a hospital in Gbagada, Lagos, a very big one.

We got into my cousin's car, and I lay back on Ruth's lap. Dumebi drove with speed. He drove like the fast and furious drivers because he had been told that I needed surgery immediately due to internal bleeding. He and his mother knew it was an emergency. Despite the hospital being far away, he was willing to take the risk and drove very fast.

At one point, I had to give my cousin my husband's number to inform him of what was happening. My husband doesn't stay in Lagos with me, so when we called him, the only thing I could say was, "Pray for me. I'm dying," because I felt life slipping away. Ruth reassured me, telling me not to say that, while I could hear her praying fervently. My aunt and Dumebi were also praying, and he continued to drive as fast as he could.

At one point, I passed out. I recall opening my eyes when we got to the hospital. They had to bring a stretcher, but the stretcher couldn't access the stairs because I needed to be taken to the first floor. Dumebi came again, lifted me, and carried me while they were still debating how to get the stretcher upstairs. He carried me to the room for them to prepare me immediately without delays. They checked my vitals and everything. They handed over the notes from the previous hospital to the doctor. As soon as he saw the notes, he was pleased that the previous doctor had provided a briefing. This helped him understand the situation quickly and decide on the next steps. They swiftly prepared me for surgery, shaving me and getting me ready. I was conscious at this point. They inserted a catheter, and then I was rolled into surgery.

Surgery

Before the surgery started, the doctor mentioned that he had concluded his shift for the day but didn't know why he had stayed around. He had just finished another surgery and was supposed to head home immediately, but he kept lingering at the hospital. He said it was clear that God wanted him to handle my surgery. He asked if I believed in God, and I said yes. He then asked, "Do you believe that you are going to make it out of this surgery?" I said yes. He assured me that he also believed I would make it through, encouraging me to stay relaxed and hopeful.

At this point, I had not been informed that I had lost my pregnancy. I was unaware of this. The doctor was simply encouraging me, saying that the surgery was necessary and that they needed to perform it. I knew I was experiencing internal bleeding and that the previous doctor had mentioned something about my tubes. Consent was obtained from my aunt, who had spoken to my husband, and the necessary deposits for the surgery were made by her.

The next thing I knew, the doctor began singing praise and worship songs. I joined him because they were songs I knew. We sang together, *"Thou art worthy, Thou art worthy, O Lord, to receive glory, honour, and power, for Thou hast created all things, and for Thy pleasure they are and were created. Thou art worthy."* As we sang, he gave me an injection, and I became unconscious.

During the surgery, while I was unconscious, I had the strangest dream. In that dream, I didn't see anyone. I just saw myself in something like a trolley, rolling around in a very beautiful, colourful place, more like a huge tunnel. It was like running into a rainbow, with green, yellow, white, and pink spirals, like a tube. I was just rolling through this tunnel filled with various beautiful colours. There were hollow sounds with little echoes, and the colours kept going round and round. It was never-ending. Sometimes it felt like I was in the clouds, then back to the rainbow, and then back to the clouds again. It was just in and out, moving from a cloudy room to a room filled with rainbow colours. Then, suddenly, it all stopped. I didn't hear anything, see anything, or see colours anymore. It just stopped.

Waking Up After Surgery

I woke up from surgery almost 18 hours later. The first person I saw beside me was my uncle's wife, Auntie Awele. I was very grateful to her for waiting. She told me that the surgery took about two or three hours. She was scared at one point because the surgery was taking quite a while. I was dazed and speechless but grateful for her staying all that time for me to come out of surgery. She said the doctor told her that the surgery was successful and that I would be fine.

Looking at her face, I couldn't really read what was going on, but I sensed that something might have happened. I looked at myself and knew it was a major surgery, but I couldn't grasp what exactly had happened. I didn't know if I still had my baby. I didn't know the details of the surgery.

My husband was notified that I was out of surgery. He said he needed to leave his workplace, but they were not giving him permission to travel.

He wanted to leave the office without permission, but I pleaded with him that it wasn't necessary. He said he would see what he could do to get that permission, and if he didn't get it, he would start heading to Lagos anyway and be AWOL.

I had internal bleeding and sensed I had lost my baby, but I wasn't sure because it hadn't been mentioned, and I didn't want to ask. I was still so weak and soon fell back asleep.

One piece of advice I gave myself at one of the lowest points of my life is this. It's important to recognise that things often become more challenging before they get easier. This is a natural part of life's journey. Every struggle we encounter contributes to our unique story, shaping us into who we are meant to be.

When we face difficulties, it can be tempting to feel disheartened or overwhelmed. However, it is crucial to maintain a positive mindset and remain strong. These challenging times are not permanent, and enduring them with resilience can lead to personal growth and strength.

Remember, everyone faces struggles at various points in their lives. You are not alone in your challenges. Take these moments as opportunities to learn and develop. By staying positive and strong, you can navigate through tough times and emerge more resilient on the other side.

So, keep your head up and continue moving forward. The difficulties you face now are merely temporary hurdles on the path to a brighter future. Stay hopeful, keep pushing, and trust that easier times are ahead.

I woke up lying on the hospital bed, dazed and confused, having been under general anaesthesia for a long time. My uncle's wife was no longer there, she must have gone back home to refresh after spending hours in the hospital. There was a tube protruding from my abdomen, creating the unsettling sensation of an unsealed wound. Why was the tube there? Why wasn't it sealed? So many questions swirled in my mind, but I lacked the strength to press the bell for the doctor or a nurse. Exhausted, I drifted back to sleep.

When I awoke, I couldn't recall how long I'd been asleep. I found myself surrounded by a doctor and nurses conducting their ward rounds, checking on patients and their progress, and answering any questions they might have. Relief washed over me at the sight of the doctor; I had so many questions that needed answers.

"I'm the doctor who performed your surgery," he said.

"Yes, I remember," I replied, my voice weak.

He asked how I was feeling. "I can't really explain," I said. "I'm just here."

Sensing my confusion and need for clarity, he took the time to explain the situation to me.

He told me that the tube was there to drain blood and fluid from my abdomen, as I still had internal blood that needed to be drained. He explained that, from time to time, the nurses would come to tilt me to the side and clean the area to ensure proper drainage. It was then that I also noticed another tube coming from my private area to help me pass urine. Looking at myself, I felt like a helpless patient. I couldn't go to the toilet by myself, and there were tubes protruding from my tummy and private area. It was overwhelming.

Noticing my distress and the pain I was in, the doctor decided to hold back additional information. He asked if I was expecting anyone to come and stay with me. I told him definitely. He said he would return later and asked the nurses to notify him when any family member arrived.

After a while, my cousin Isioma came to stay with me in the hospital. She is a few years older than me and is like an elder sister. My uncle and his wife had instructed her to stay with me to provide the necessary assistance. When she arrived, the doctor was notified, and he came back to speak with me.

With Isioma by my side, the doctor gently explained that I had lost a tube, which was why I was bleeding. I had also lost the baby. I froze. I couldn't believe that I had lost the pregnancy. I froze because my fears were confirmed. It was the last thing I had anticipated for myself, and I felt a profound sadness engulf me.

I was broken!

> *"Success is not final; failure is not fatal: It is the courage to continue that counts."*
>
> **— Winston Churchill**

Chapter 3

Post-Surgery

The doctor tried to reassure me. He told me that, in a way, I was fortunate because if I hadn't arrived when I did, I might have lost my life. He said that since I was alive, there was hope for me to have another baby. He mentioned that many women who have lost a tube still go on to have children, so losing a tube wasn't the end of the world.

When I asked him what had happened, he told me it was an ectopic pregnancy. This was the first time I had ever heard that term. I had no idea what an ectopic pregnancy was; it was a concept I had never encountered before.

After the doctor left, I looked up "ectopic pregnancy" on Google. The information I found was overwhelming. My mood shifted dramatically, and my hope was dashed. An ectopic pregnancy occurs when a fertilised egg implants outside the uterus, most commonly in the fallopian tube. The fallopian tube isn't made to hold a growing embryo. This condition can lead to bleeding in the birth parent.

An ectopic pregnancy is a life-threatening condition that requires emergency treatment. Ectopic pregnancies can become life-threatening, especially if the fallopian tube breaks (ruptures). This can cause severe bleeding, infection, and sometimes death. It is a medical emergency that must be treated quickly. Some causes could be an irregularly-shaped fallopian tube or a growth blocking the fallopian tube; in my case, I also had a fibroid, as the doctor informed me.

I felt alone in the world, pained, and abandoned.

I couldn't understand why this was happening to me. It seemed so unfair—I tried to live a decent life, and yet I felt like I didn't deserve this.

It was incredibly painful. After marrying, getting pregnant shortly after, and then losing the pregnancy—it all seemed too much. I wasn't coping well, and I cried intermittently. My cousin Isioma did everything she could to console me, but the hurt was deep.

My Husband's Arrives

That evening, my husband arrived from Delta State. I was happy to see him, but I was also in tears. He tried to calm me down, explaining that he had left his workplace without permission. He couldn't accept that his workplace was delaying his leave, especially given the emergency with his wife. This was our first pregnancy, and they were adamant about not understanding that he needed to be with his wife. I was genuinely grateful that he managed to make it, but my tears did not stop. I cried continuously—morning, afternoon, and night. My husband did everything he could to comfort me.

I had not yet told my parents about the surgery, so my husband made the call. They were completely devastated. My mother said she would travel from Owerri to Lagos, but I told her that it wasn't necessary, as it was a long trip and I already had people around me who had been very helpful. I didn't want my mother to witness my daily crying, as it would break her heart.

The dressing of the surgery site and the area with the tube was something I would never forget; it was always very painful. Every time they came to change the dressing, they had to tilt me to drain the blood from the tubes, and it seemed like the blood in my system was endless. They had to drain the blood twice a day, in the morning and evening.

I remember having that tube for about a week, I think. I was still in the emergency ward, and the doctor kept coming to check on me, stating that I needed to remain there due to my fragile state, which required close observation. Each morning, the routine involved tilting me to drain the blood, cleaning the surgery area, and changing the bag from my private area if it was full. They even showed my husband how to change it, just in case it got full and there was no one else around.

Hospital admission was something I detested, but I had to remain there for proper care. One morning, I cried uncontrollably again, and despite my husband's attempts to console me, I told him to find another wife and that there was no need for him to wait for me. I had researched ectopic pregnancy and knew that while my chances of having children were still there, it might take time.

My husband said something surprising and deeply reassuring. He said, "I didn't marry you for babies. I married you for love. I married you because I love you. I married you for companionship and for us, not for babies. If the babies come, they are a blessing and an addition to us. And if God decides they won't come, no problem. We will stay together."

His words were incredibly supportive and

reminded me of how fortunate I was to have him in my life. Although my crying did not stop entirely, it was less frequent because he was there, continually reassuring me that I would be fine.

I recall an elderly nurse who came one day and saw my husband wiping away my tears. She asked what was going on, and he told her about my concerns and my belief that I would not be able to have children in a timely manner. To my surprise, she opened her blouse and showed me a scar similar to mine from a major surgery. She had also had an ectopic pregnancy and lost a tube, but she had five children. She told me, "Who told you that you won't be able to have children? You will be able to have children. Eat the right food, get enough rest, keep the right habits, and keep praying. Children will come. I have five children despite having an ectopic pregnancy. So don't think you won't be able to have babies on your own.

Hope is Not Lost

I want to encourage women who are holding on to hope after experiencing something like this. I met a woman who had an ectopic pregnancy and went on to have five children without any fertility procedures. The first child took about five to six years to arrive, but once the first child was born, the others followed almost immediately. Despite losing a tube, she was able to have five children. There are also several medical procedures and methods for having children; some work after the first try, and some require several attempts. I also know of others who have had failed attempts. It all depends on personal circumstances. Hope is never lost!

This renewed my hope. My crying decreased drastically, and I was profoundly grateful to be alive. For the first time, I felt a deep sense of gratitude for my life. My faith and hope in God began to return. Although I was broken and in pain, I was thankful that I had not turned away from my faith or spoken any rebellious words. I remained silent, and after hearing that woman's testimony, my hope was reignited, especially with my husband by my side, praying constantly.

On the seventh day, a nurse came to drain the

blood from the tube again. This time, she noticed that only a little bit of water came out, and no more blood. They decided it was time to remove the tube from my stomach. The doctor came to check and confirm what the nurses had said. He examined me, tilted me, and verified that no more blood was coming out. He informed me that they would be removing the tube that day.

I asked him if it would be painful, and he assured me it wouldn't be too painful, just a little bit of discomfort. I didn't entirely believe him, as this was a sizable tube sticking out of my stomach. I wondered how removing it could possibly be painless. I asked if they would need to perform another surgery to remove the tube, but he said no, it would be removed manually without surgery.

When the time came for the nurse to remove the tube, I felt overwhelmed by the continual pain I was experiencing. I had already endured significant pain before the surgery, surgery pain, and post-surgery pain, and now I was facing the removal of yet another tube. It was all too much to bear, and I started crying again.

However, the nurse was incredibly experienced and calming. She told me stories to distract me while she gradually pulled out the tube. Although I felt a lot of pain, it wasn't as severe as I had anticipated, thanks to her skill. Once the tube was out, the area was dressed with a plaster. I was told that the incision would gradually heal on its own. It seemed strange to me that I wasn't going to have another surgery to close the hole; I was simply told that it would seal up on its own over time. They would continue to dress it until it healed.

After a few days, I noticed that the incision was indeed healing. I was cleared to go home, but with restrictions. I was advised not to engage in any strenuous activities and to avoid taking a proper bath; I could only clean up. The stitches used were not dissolvable and would need to be removed once the wound had healed. I was required to visit the clinic twice a week for dressing changes and to check the healing progress.

My aunt and her family, as well as my uncle,

visited almost every day. I was grateful for their support. My uncle and his wife covered the initial deposit for my surgery, and when my husband offered to reimburse them, they refused to accept it. Consequently, my husband took care of the remaining hospital bills. I stayed in the hospital for about three weeks.

When I returned to my uncle's house, my husband had to go back to work. Thankfully, his immediate boss made a case for him, and he was not penalised for leaving. I received all the love, support, and help from my uncle's family and children; Nnamdi, Dumebi, Daisy and also from Isioma. About a month later, I was told it was time to remove the stitches from the surgery. The removal was far from pleasant. It was a painful experience, and the nurse was not as careful as I would have hoped. After the stitches were removed, I returned home, feeling both relieved and exhausted.

Despite the precautions and medication, I was given, and the advice to ensure that water didn't touch the surgery area for at least a week or two, I was careful to follow the instructions. However, a few days after the stitches were removed, I started to notice swelling around the surgery area. I had to return to the hospital, where I was informed that some of the threads from the stitches had not been removed properly, which caused the swelling.

I could hardly bear the thought of enduring more pain. Why had the nurse not removed the stitches correctly? This oversight meant I had to return to the hospital three times a week for the remaining stitches to be removed. The swelling was addressed by an experienced matron who managed to remove the stitches that had been left behind in the swollen area. She explained that the previous nurse had not done a thorough job but reassured me that she would take care of the situation.

From that point on, she removed the remaining stitches from the swollen parts, advising me to visit again if any other areas swelled up. This process took another week because the swelling kept recurring, requiring further visits to remove the stitches left behind. The swelling was due to threads from the stitches that had remained embedded in my skin.

After another week, the area was finally clean, and I began to heal properly. The surgery site was healing well without any further swelling. I was grateful to the nurse, who had become a personal friend. We prayed together, and she assured me that one day I would definitely have children. She asked me never to forget to tell her when that happened.

> *"Hope is being able to see that there is light despite all of the darkness"*
>
> **— Desmond Tutu**

Chapter 4

Recovery

Questions whirred through my mind, relentless and unyielding: Why me? Why did this pain have to be my burden? What have I done to deserve this? Was I destined to be one of the few who would endure such suffering and uncertainty, only to wonder if I would ever be able to have a child again?

These questions popped up with jarring frequency, and no answers seemed forthcoming. The constant hospital visits were necessary to ensure my well-being, but they felt overwhelmingly taxing. The absence of a normal routine, such as work, left me with little to distract myself from my plight.

I remained in this state of turmoil until, after two months, a semblance of normalcy began to reappear. My colleagues' visits provided a sliver of solace and sanity amidst the chaos. Yet, a nagging question persisted in my mind: if I continued down this path of despair, might I succumb to depression?

This led me to a profound self-examination: *Where had my faith gone?* I questioned the state of my relationship with God and whether I would allow my current suffering to undermine it. In response, I began immersing myself in Scripture, seeking comfort in inspirational books and Kingdom literature designed to uplift and sustain me.

In such challenging times, it's crucial to discover what brings you comfort—be it movies, socialising with friends, or simply talking to loved ones. My options were limited due to my physical constraints: the pain restricted my mobility, and public transport was out of the question. Yet, despite these limitations, it was the Scriptures, along with the unwavering support of my spouse, family, and close friends, that kept me afloat.

Through reading and reflection, I found reassurance in the belief that God's love remained constant, despite the trials I faced. I came to understand that trials are not permanent but are often precursors to greater things. They are meant to strengthen us and pave the way for a brighter future.

Beauty Amidst the Thorns

In every challenging situation, there is always an opportunity to discover something positive. Just as roses have thorns but are still admired for their beauty, so too does life present a complex mixture of pain and beauty. It is easy to become consumed by the difficulties and struggles we face, but if we take a step back, we can often find valuable lessons and moments of joy hidden within the hardship.

Embracing this perspective requires us to look beyond the immediate discomfort and seek out the silver linings. Pain and adversity can act as catalysts for personal growth, offering us new insights and strengths we might not have discovered otherwise. By acknowledging and appreciating the small victories and the positive aspects of our experiences, we shift our focus from what we lack to what we can gain.

Life's trials are not purely negative; they are interwoven with opportunities for beauty, transformation, and resilience. Just as a rose, despite its thorns, remains a symbol of grace and elegance, our struggles can lead us to a deeper appreciation of life's beauty. It's about finding and celebrating these moments of light, even when surrounded by darkness.

I had to grasp this truth through the Scriptures. Psalm 23 tells us, "Even though I walk through the valley of the shadow of death, I will fear no evil." This verse taught me that traversing through the valley of shadows, enduring pain, tribulation, and struggle, is part of life. Yet, God assures me of His presence, promising that His rod and staff will comfort me. This assurance kept me going.

I began to feel better. My workplace granted me an extension, so I ended up spending about three months at home before returning. My diet was carefully considered, and I was unable to perform any physical tasks. I could barely manage to do anything because, after all, it was major surgery, and I was healing both physically and spiritually.

On one of these beautiful days, my husband, who had returned to his station, called me. He reassured me of his love and reminded me that our marriage was not contingent on what we could gain or achieve together, nor on the children that might come. He emphasised that he loved me for who I am, and my presence in his life meant more to him than anything else in the world. I felt immense happiness and reassurance knowing that the man who had taken me down the aisle still cared deeply for me.

Despite having lost a tube, I heard many stories of women who faced broken marriages due to their hospitalisation and abandonment by their spouses.

My experience was quite the opposite. I had a man who cared deeply, who was always reassuring me of his support. I also had wonderful parents who were there for me, praying and checking in regularly. My mother, a devoted prayer warrior, continued to pray and reassure me that everything would be okay. My siblings were supportive, as were my cousins. I was staying at my uncle's house in Lagos with his family, and they treated me with kindness and respect. My uncle and his wife never made me feel any less than cherished.

Strength From Scriptures

When you are going through difficult life events, surround yourself with the best people and distance yourself from toxic influences. If someone doesn't contribute positively to your well-being, it's best to quietly stay away. Do not dwell on the past. Spiritual healing is far more important than physical healing. This was a realisation I came to during my surgery recovery. Even though my surgical site was healing well, I was still grappling with my emotions. I had intermittent periods where

I cried uncontrollably, feeling as though a part of me was missing. Losing a tube made me feel incomplete, as though something essential was lacking within me.

However, I found reassurance in the Scriptures, which helped me stay strong and positive. I guided myself with Bible verses before bedtime and prayers in the morning. This routine was instrumental in preventing me from falling into depression. While it may sound unusual to some, I found that Scripture was a powerful tool to guard against negativity and despair. The word of God played a significant role in my life, offering countless reassuring verses that strengthened me during difficult times. I often felt as though the Bible was like my angel book, providing support alongside the love and care of those around me.

One of the beautiful moments came when my cousin started planning for my return to the office. Initially, I thought she was being a bit overzealous. She insisted I needed to think about resuming work and advised me to reconsider my wardrobe. She pointed out that trousers and belts might not be suitable for me at the moment. Instead, she suggested opting for simple, corporate dresses that wouldn't cling to my abdominal area.

I was touched by her thoughtfulness. Fortunately, Isioma is a talented seamstress, and her plan became a welcome distraction for me. We went shopping for fabrics and materials, and she began making me a collection of lovely, simple office dresses. We looked through magazines to find styles that would be appropriate for my return to work. I was immensely grateful, not only for the beautiful dresses but also for the fact that I didn't have to pay much for them—just a small amount for the materials.

This planning and preparation for my return to the office were significant in my healing process, contributing to my overall sense of well-being and happiness.

From Pain To Purpose

When you're in the process of healing, whether from physical surgery or emotional distress, immersing yourself in creative activities can be incredibly beneficial. Engaging in something creative serves as a powerful distraction from your pain, helping to redirect your thoughts and energy. Instead of being consumed by the discomfort or sadness of your situation, you channel your focus into something productive and imaginative.

This shift in focus not only provides a mental break from the constant rumination over your suffering but also fosters a sense of accomplishment and joy. Creative pursuits, such as painting, writing, crafting, or even organising your environment, can offer therapeutic benefits. They allow you to express your emotions in a constructive manner and can significantly lift your mood.

Moreover, the process of creating something—whether it's a piece of art, a new recipe, or a personal project—can help you regain a sense of normalcy and control. It shifts your attention from what you've lost or are enduring to what you can build or achieve. This active engagement with creativity often leads to a more positive outlook and can significantly enhance your overall well-being during recovery.

Picking out styles, choosing materials, and planning for my return to work were major changes in my mindset. These activities provided a welcome distraction and helped me maintain a positive outlook.

I began to notice that I was feeling better. I could take longer walks and overall felt much improved. As I approached my resumption day, I realised I hadn't considered something important—shoes!

I'm usually very adept at wearing high-heeled shoes. I'm a corporate lady who loves being on heels. However, this time, my wardrobe had to shift. I had to forego my beloved heels and switch to flat shoes, which I detested. But I had no choice; I was instructed to wear flat shoes until I was completely free from the pain of the surgery.

So, another trip to the market with my cousin was in order. We chose shoes in black, brown, dark blue, and oxblood—colours permitted in the office. Flashy colours like yellow or red were off-limits. We managed to find flat shoes that suited my tastes for my return to work.

The day before my resumption, which was a Sunday, I went to church, prayed, and felt happy. However, a wave of anxiety soon followed. I was plagued by questions: Would I stay in the marketing department? Would I meet my targets? Would people question me? Would I fit in again? Could I live up to my job expectations? Honestly, I wasn't keen on resuming.

I recalled my uncle's wife advising me to brace myself for resumption, take things easy at work, and remember that everything would turn out fine. Her words provided some reassurance. I hesitated to call my husband, feeling it might disturb him. Strangely, just when I thought I shouldn't call him, he called me. He remembered that my resumption was the next day, encouraged me, and we prayed together over the phone. He reminded me that it would be a step-by-step process and hoped that soon I could relocate to Asaba to be closer to him. His support was exactly what I needed.

Once I resumed work, I resolved to focus more on relocating to join my husband in Asaba. Although I was contemplating resignation, my husband helped me see that now was not the time to resign but to think about moving. With his encouragement, I went to bed feeling reassured and happy, prayed, and had a restful sleep.

"The Lord will perfect that which concerneth me."

— Psalm 138:8

Chapter 5

Back to Work

Returning to work after a three-month hiatus was a surprisingly uplifting experience. I was greeted with the warm, reassuring embrace of my colleagues, their genuine joy at my return palpable in every smile and handshake. The atmosphere buzzed with kindness and support, as everyone went out of their way to assist me with anything I needed. Their thoughtful advice and friendly demeanour made me feel right at home. My manager, too, was visibly pleased to have me back, offering me the comforting reassurance to take things at my own pace. As I settled into my first day back, I found myself enveloped in a cocoon of goodwill and encouragement, making the transition back to work not only manageable but genuinely heartening.

Gradually, I started adapting to the things I had missed—going to the market to seek out clients and returning to complete my call notes. I managed these tasks with relative ease and had access to the branch vehicle, which was helpful given my recent recovery.

Coping with Work Pressures

One fateful day, we were summoned by our manager who was furious about our failure to meet targets. Our branch's productivity was disappointingly low. He kept us standing throughout his tirade, berating us for our lack of results. The threats and his high-pitched tone made us feel as though we were accomplishing nothing. I felt disheartened that, despite my recent return and three-months absence, I was subjected to such harsh criticism. I was feeling dizzy but dared not interrupt his scolding.

The next thing I knew, I was collapsing. My colleagues later informed me that I had fainted briefly due to the stress of standing for an extended period. The pressure from the situation must have contributed to my collapse. They helped me calm down and advised me to go home early to rest. My colleagues expressed their frustration, suggesting that the manager should have been more considerate and allowed us to sit during his address.

At that moment, all I could think about was how I would manage the pressures of my marketing job. The strain of recovering from surgery and being away from my spouse made everything more challenging. The following day, I returned to the office, but there was no preferential treatment for what had happened. It was business as usual. I spent the morning following up with the Human Resources department about my transfer to join my husband in Asaba, but the response remained unchanged: there were still no openings available.

Fingers crossed, I kept praying and believing in God, along with my husband, that we would successfully navigate this challenge. Two weeks later, after the incident where I collapsed in the office, something happened.

Upon arriving at the office, we heard whispers in the corridor and overheard the Secretary mention that our manager had been fired. It was a shock. Although I knew he was very harsh and had high expectations, I couldn't ignore that he was also a hardworking person. I don't feel good about anyone being fired, regardless of how they treated me. It's never something I wish upon anyone.

After a while, we gathered in the manager's office where he informed us that he had been asked to leave, attributing it to our branch's poor performance. He expressed that the blame for the branch's underachievement was being directed at the marketing team. He packed up his belongings and cleared his desk, and we bid him farewell. It was painful because we hadn't anticipated this outcome. He was a family man with children, and it is never ideal for anyone to lose their employment.

Dealing with a Toxic Work Environment

Many people find it incredibly challenging to cope with a toxic work environment, to the extent that it affects their mental health and the way they treat those around them. A toxic workplace can be detrimental, causing significant stress and anxiety.

One of the key things I have always made sure to avoid is letting bitterness and anger take root in my life. Even when faced with a difficult or unjust boss, I never allowed myself to harbour ill will or wish harm upon them. Herein lies an important lesson: the moment you allow bitterness to take hold due to the way someone treats you, it acts like a poison, impacting your mental well-being.

To navigate such a difficult situation, it is vital to take proactive steps. Firstly, pray to find inner peace. Additionally, seeking professional help, can provide valuable support and guidance. It is important to devise a strategy to leave the toxic environment, whether that means finding a new job or addressing the issues through appropriate channels within your current organisation.

Remember, the way you are treated in a toxic workplace does not define you. It reflects solely on the perpetrator and their own issues. Maintaining your integrity and positive outlook is crucial. By refusing to let bitterness and anger consume you, you protect your mental health and ensure that you continue to treat others with kindness and respect.

New Management

Two days later, a new manager was appointed—this time a woman. She was indeed a breath of fresh air. Our first meeting with her revealed a completely different approach to marketing. She was a firm believer in daily meetings and was an excellent motivator.

Whereas we previously thought our old boss was hardworking, we now saw a leader who was a true go-getter. She was results-oriented which significantly increased the branch's client base and brought in substantial revenue. Her leadership inspired us to embrace a new mindset. We approached marketing with renewed energy and innovative ideas, encouraged by her example.

Under her guidance, there were significant changes: she shuffled personnel, moving some from customer service to marketing and vice versa. This rejuvenated the branch, leading to a period of outstanding performance and achievement of targets.

Good News of My Transfer

One fateful morning, after our usual meeting, our boss decided to attend a general meeting of all branch managers at the head office. She returned a few hours later and asked someone to fetch me. When I arrived at her office, she was visibly upset. I wondered what I could have done to upset her so much. She told me she was unhappy and felt that I didn't like her, which was untrue. I asked her to clarify what I had done wrong, as I was genuinely clueless. I had always admired her both personally and for her leadership style, which was a blend of carrot and stick. She rebuked yet encouraged.

She expressed her frustration, saying, "Pamela, why would you decide to leave my branch now that I've just joined? I was so happy to have you here, and now it seems you're leaving." I explained that my plans to relocate to be with my husband had been in place long before she was assigned to our branch. To make her understand my situation, I showed her the scar from my major surgery and shared my recovery experience. We ended up crying together, holding hands.

She acknowledged her pain at losing me from her team but was also happy that I would finally be joining my husband, who had been waiting for me. She delivered the joyous news that my transfer had been approved and that I would be advised shortly by the head office. Despite her initial devastation upon learning about my transfer, understanding the full story behind it made her happy to release me.

She requested my husband's phone number and called him to share the good news. He was delighted, and she encouraged him to take care of me as I would soon be joining him. Returning to my desk, I felt overjoyed knowing that I would finally be moving to Asaba to live with my dear husband. Our home would no longer be filled with the separation that the distance brought but with renewed hope, peace, and joy.

My husband and I discussed what adjustments we could make to the house to ensure my comfort upon my arrival. This was truly one of the best days at work. It was hard to believe that what I had waited for so long was finally happening, exactly two years after my wedding. I was incredibly grateful that my dream of relocating to be with my husband was finally coming true. My friends Wale and Loye were so happy for me and took turns giving me an early send-off treat.

I was given two weeks to tidy up my work, hand over my accounts to my colleagues, and prepare for my move to Asaba. I thanked God, as my long-awaited dream to be with my husband was about to be realised.

> *"It's not about ideas; it's about making ideas happen."*
>
> **—Scott Belsky**

Chapter 6

At Last

The last two weeks in the office before my move to Asaba were the most exhilarating of my career. With the exciting prospect of finally joining my husband two years after our wedding, I found a renewed sense of purpose. Every task was a joy as I meticulously handed over my accounts to my colleagues. I took pride in personally introducing them to my clients and explaining that I would be relocating to be with my husband. The responses were mixed—some clients shared in my happiness, while others were less thrilled about having a new relationship manager. Despite this, the anticipation of reuniting with my husband filled each day with hope and excitement, making these final weeks truly unforgettable.

But this is what comes with the job, I told some of them. I can't be your relationship manager forever. Someday I may be transferred, voluntarily or involuntarily. This time, it's a voluntary transfer as it's necessary for me to join my husband.

Back home, packing my things gradually was quite a task. Despite the short time I had spent with my uncle, I had acquired quite a lot: new office attire, various bags, and shoes. Thanks to my cousins who helped me with the thorough packing, the first batch of my belongings was sent through courier services to my husband. This would help me travel light when it was time for me to move.

On that beautiful morning, it was time for me to submit my final handover and farewell letter to my colleagues. It was a day of mixed feelings, as most of my colleagues were not happy about my departure. They understood, though, that meeting my husband was the best thing for me. The office was quite gloomy, especially my new manager, who was reluctant to let me go. We talked at length, and she wished me well.

My colleagues and I spent some time together in the office as they had organised a send-off party for me, exchanging gifts and words of encouragement. They said wonderful things about me and how good it had been to work with me. I cried as I heard my colleagues share their kind words. It was refreshing to hear the positive things they were going to miss about me. I acknowledged that we all have our flaws and that I tried to be as good as possible. I asked them to forgive me for any offence I might have caused, explaining that it was never personal, just work-related. They prayed for me and wished me well, and I did the same for them.

Getting back home, I felt a sigh of relief. I told myself, "Finally, it's time to go to Asaba to be with my husband." It was a difficult night's sleep because I was both excited and anxious. I was also going to miss my uncle and his wonderful family. The excitement was about meeting my husband, while the anxiety stemmed from starting work with a new set of people and building new relationships. Nevertheless, I was ready to face it, as being with my husband had always been my dream.

The next morning, on the eventful day, my uncle and cousin took me to the station. My cousin accompanied him to pay for my ticket, and then they bid me farewell. As I waited for the bus to load, my husband called, filled with excitement. The joy in his voice and the thought of us being together again was palpable. I told him we would see each other in a few hours. The journey from Lagos to Asaba takes about seven hours on a day with little traffic.

The journey commenced at about 8:50 am. At intervals, I spoke with my husband. I arrived in Asaba at about 3 pm, with my loving husband already waiting at the park. It was indeed the best day of my life. We held each other so tightly and didn't want to let go. I cried like a baby, feeling as if a heavy burden had been lifted from my chest. He looked at me with tears in his eyes and said, "You've lost a lot of weight. But don't worry, everything is fine." His assurance meant the world to me. After my things were brought down from the bus, we headed straight home.

Stepping into the house, we prayed, and I told God that my coming into this home would be the start of greater and better things for myself and my husband. I was to resume work in two days, as it was Thursday when I arrived. So, I had Friday and the weekend to prepare for my new job starting on Monday.

In the evening, after taking a shower and a short nap, my husband took me out to one of the nicest, coolest places where we could eat the popular "nkwobi," a local delicacy made of cow meat with lots of spice and pepper. We enjoyed it with a chilled bottle of malt, my favourite drink. I felt incredibly happy; I couldn't remember the last time I had hung out like this. Lagos had hardly given me the time to visit nice places, except for eateries and the beach. However, in Asaba, there were many such spots where one could sit out, enjoy the fresh air, have a chilled drink, and eat good food—fried meat, wild meat, pepper soup, or barbecue fish and meat. It was really nice.

We spent the time talking about work and how I was feeling mentally and physically. Indeed, it was another very good evening. We got back home feeling really happy, filled with new expectations and new hope.

Your 'At Last' Moment is Coming

Every now and then, there comes a moment when, at long last, our dreams come to fruition, even if it happens after a prolonged period of waiting and perseverance. This was my 'at last' moment – the time when my hopes to be with my husband were finally realised.

Whatever challenges you are facing, remember that delays are not your destiny. The waiting period you are enduring will ultimately pay off. Your 'at last' moment is on its way, perhaps sooner than you anticipate.

Stay faithful and committed throughout the

process, and do not lose heart. It is essential to remain resilient and steadfast, trusting that your time will come. Just as my dreams were realised, so too will yours be, in the fullness of time.

Keep the faith, continue to work diligently, and maintain a positive outlook. The journey may be arduous, but the reward will be worth the wait. Your 'at last' moment is approaching, bringing with it the fulfilment of your dreams and the realisation of your hard work and dedication.

Starting My New Job

On Monday, the anticipated day, I arrived at the office to meet a sea of new faces. I asked for the Head of Operations, who I was supposed to report to. It turned out to be a man, not a woman as I had initially thought. He acknowledged receiving the email about my transfer and warmly welcomed me. During their usual morning meeting, I was introduced to all the staff and security personnel. The branch was smaller compared to my previous branch in Lagos, which had over 30 staff members. This branch had fewer than 30 staff, but it was a beautiful branch nonetheless. My workstation was already prepared for me.

This role was a new challenge as I had been in the marketing department in Lagos. The opening I received in Asaba was for customer service. Human Resources deemed it fit for me to switch to customer service due to the nature of the surgery I had undergone. They felt it was better for me to work in the branch rather than going out looking for clients. I was very grateful for that consideration.

My new colleague and friend Chinwe in customer service was there to guide me through my new responsibilities. We developed a very good working relationship. I quickly learned how to open accounts for customers, check balances, handle queries and complaints, process debit card requests, handle chequebook requests, reactivate dormant accounts, and manage transaction alert requests. We also handled the Know Your Customer (KYC) updates. The customer service department was busy and involved a lot of document filing, but the advantage was that I got to sit all day instead of going out to find clients.

I adapted quickly to the customer service role and eventually became the head of the department after about three years. My friend was transferred to another branch, where she also headed the customer service unit. As Head of Customer Service, I worked with new subordinates and was responsible for coaching them, which I did joyfully.

Although my primary role was Head of Customer Service, I often kept an eye on the cash region. Sometimes, I would help them if their balances were off, checking their transactions to find errors that might have led to an overage or shortage.

This process is known as a "call-over." A call-over involves printing out the transactions a particular cashier has done for the day and comparing those transactions on the printouts to the physical withdrawal or deposit documents to check for errors. I frequently performed this task and often identified errors, which helped the cashiers balance their accounts in no time.

A Slight Shift in Work Roles

One day, a nearby branch experienced a staff layoff, and there was a delay in getting a replacement. I was asked to quickly go to that branch to cover for the staff member who had been dismissed. This staff member was the Head of Cash, also referred to as Head Teller in some banks. So, I was sent to the nearby branch to fill in for that position. I worked there for about two weeks while waiting for the bank to find a replacement.

Even though it was a new role for me, I managed well because I had a good understanding of the operations. I helped the branch close and balance each day for the next two weeks. During this time, I heard that someone had been brought in to occupy my position at my original branch. I was initially unhappy and confused, thinking my transfer was temporary. I dismissed the rumour, believing the new person was a temporary replacement while I was away.

However, it turned out that the position was permanently filled. When I returned to my branch and checked the portal, I saw that this person's role had been changed to my previous role, which was Head of Customer Service, and mine was undefined as my name was no longer part of the branch complement. I just couldn't understand it. I asked questions to understand why I had been treated this way but received no answers. I was devastated. It felt as if I had been used and discarded. In my years of banking, I had never heard of such a move without formal notification or explanation. I knew the bank was laying off staff, and everyone was clamouring for a permanent position, which I had before I was asked to help the other branch.

I cried and felt frustrated because I had no intention of moving into the cash role permanently. Moreover, the branch I was covering had already found a permanent replacement for the position. Now, my position had been taken over, leaving me in limbo. It was one of the worst days of my life, and many thoughts ran through my mind.

But something inside me reminded me of God's love and the scriptures that say, "I will not be put to shame," and "When men revile and persecute you and say all kinds of evil against you falsely, rejoice." The scriptures reassured me that God had not forgotten me.

My husband and I prayed endlessly. After the prayers, I felt a sense of peace. I knew that everything would be alright. Everything would be fine for those who believe. I'm a strong believer that when things happen, they happen for a reason. But sometimes, as humans, we tend to forget that when things happen to us, God has a lesson or something to teach us. Another thing I learned from this is that God has bigger and better plans for us than we could ever imagine.

Returning to the office the next day, I received a call from my regional manager. He informed me that I would be assisting the regional support staff in Asaba. Wow! What a testimony, what an elevation, what a great turnaround of events for me. Here I was, upset over a Head of Customer Service position being taken away. Little did I know that I was being prepared for bigger opportunities. I was now assisting with regional work, collaborating with the regional support staff. We both reported to the regional manager, helping to collect reports, pass information, assist with scorecard analysis, and perform monthly analyses of the zone.

One thing I started doing was sending inspirational messages every morning to everyone in the zone. I continued this practice for years until I left the bank. I was so happy and thanked God, telling Him that He had wiped the tears from my eyes. My regional manager assured me that I was good enough to do the job. The next day, I moved to the next branch to work with the regional support staff. I already had a space carved out for me, and work commenced. The same people who I had previously worked with and reported, now render their reports to me, which I would collate and submit to the region Manager.

I won't lie—I did feel a bit resentful at first towards those I thought were responsible for removing me from my position. But in the long run, I realised they hadn't removed me; God had allowed it to happen so that I could move on to bigger and better things. Working in the region exposed me to a wealth of reports and knowledge that I had not gained during my years working in the bank. Often, even when the support staff went on leave, I would cover for them and handle the job very well. I was extremely grateful to God as I enjoyed the new role, which also came with a lot of respect. I no longer had to deal with the noisy banking hall and could concentrate on zonal analysis reporting to the regional manager.

> *"The size of your dream must always exceed your current capacity."*
>
> **—Jim Rohn**

Chapter 7

Delays won't be Denials

One thing that remained was the fact that I had not been promoted. I was given higher responsibilities and occupied higher positions but remained on the same grade. This was about my seventh year in the bank. Every year after I joined, the bank released promotion lists, and I never got promoted. Year two, three, four and five—each year, I would meet my targets, make a difference, and receive praise and accolades for my versatility. Yet, promotion lists came and went, and I was never on them. I kept wondering what was going on, putting in my best and doing exceptionally well, but still, no promotion.

At intervals, I talked to God, asking why I was moved to greater responsibilities and better positions but remained on the same grade. It was as if I wasn't hearing from God regarding that. I didn't hear anything. I remained in the same position, and no promotion came, despite my exceptional performance.

After a year, the bank decided to scrap the role of regional support. This became another time of panic for me, and I thought, "God, you brought me to this position, and now it's going to be scrapped. Is this a repeat of the events that happened before?" However, God was faithful. One of the branches had an opening for a Head Teller, also known as Head of Cash in some banks. That was how I became Head of Cash.

Recall, that my initial background was in marketing; then I moved to customer service and rose to Head of Customer Service. Ideally, I was supposed to get a Head of Customer Service position. But no, God placed me as Head of Cash, a role I was familiar with from my relief work as regional support. An opening came up, and I became Head of Cash in Asaba. God was so faithful that I didn't have to leave Asaba. The only times I left Asaba were for regional relief work. My entire work time was in Asaba. I was grateful because I couldn't bear the thought of staying away from my husband again.

Great Daughter

"*Ada Úkwú*," my mother calls out whenever I've done something truly exceptional or made a remarkable contribution to our family. It's a name that has grown into a cherished part of who I am. The words mean "*Great Daughter*," and they resonate deeply with me. Each time she says it, I feel a swell of pride and love, knowing that I've made a meaningful impact. This name is not just a label but a reflection of the love and appreciation that binds our family together, and it has become a source of personal significance and joy in my life.

My parents have always been incredibly proud of me, in general. I didn't let the fact that I didn't have children of my own stop me from being helpful and supportive. I refused to let the absence of my own children hinder me from showing love and care to those with kids. I've witnessed people shut their hearts to helping expectant mothers or anyone with children because they believe they are being punished for not having their own. However, this never deterred me from being a valuable contributor to progress and growth, both within my family and beyond. I took on projects and completed them diligently, regardless of my gender. I did what I knew was right and pleasing to God, honouring my parents and continuing to do so, knowing that such respect would ensure my days are long and fulfilling.

Don't Shut Yourself

Here are some words of encouragement to you—whether you are a sister, a mother, an aunt, or an uncle who is waiting to have a child. Please don't close yourself off from the world or shy away from helping others simply because you're still on your own journey to parenthood. It's important to continue being a beacon of support and kindness, no matter your circumstances. Embrace the opportunity to contribute positively to the lives of those around you. By staying engaged and compassionate, you not only honour your own values but also bring joy and support to others. Keep doing what you know is right and what pleases God, and trust that your efforts will be recognised and rewarded in ways you may not yet foresee.

After all, you have your life because God gave it to you. My mum and I continue to chat on the phone, and she tells me about the things they've been able to purchase with the funds I've sent them. As usual, my dad is in the background, saying, "Thank you o. We received it o. God bless you o. May you never lack o. You are indeed a blessing to us o. May God grant you children who will honour you as you honour us." These are my parents' words every time I call them or do something, whether small or significant, for the family. My parents are retired and they gave me all that was required when they were in active service. It's right for me to be there for them and support them in the little way I can.

I come from a close-knit family of five children: two girls and three boys. The order is as follows: Chuks is after me, followed by Shirley, then Uche, and the youngest is Chiedu. We maintain our bond through a WhatsApp group where we discuss daily matters. While we do have our disagreements, like any regular family, we also share many good times. The most important thing is that we always reconcile quickly after any arguments. As "ADA ÚKWÚ," the great daughter, the first daughter and first child of my mum, I make it a priority to keep the peace and ensure that we remain united. I stay involved in my siblings' lives, supporting them through their struggles and celebrating their victories. I will never abandon any of them because, even though I don't yet have children of my own, I view my siblings as my own children.

My siblings are deeply concerned about my not having a child. I understand how worried and concerned they are, and they do not hesitate to show me that they are praying for me.

For my parents and siblings, it's all about love and supportive conversations.

However, some people would ask, "What are you waiting for? Have you seen a doctor? Time is running out." These are some of the things people say to me, and I look at them, feeling they lack understanding. Do they think I'm not concerned about having a child? Do they think it doesn't trouble me? It seems to me that it's not their place to speak to me in that manner, but that's just the nature of society and what it entails.

I remember an aunt who once brought a so called Pastor to pray for me. After the prayers, he delivered a 'revelation' that had no relevance to my condition. There's a common misconception that if you don't have a child or if it takes a long time, it might be due to having had a series of abortions. Unfortunately, this was not my case. When the pastor—or whatever he claimed to be—suggested that I should ask God for forgiveness for an abortion, I immediately intervened. I informed my aunt that this man was not genuine because I had never had an abortion, nor had I ever been pregnant again after my surgery.

So, I briskly walked out of that prayer session.

This can never remove the fact that there are genuine Pastors and men of God and I respect the anointing over their lives and ministry.

Create Boundaries

When we are navigating through challenging times, it's crucial to be extremely discerning about the people we allow into our lives. The individuals we choose to surround ourselves with can significantly influence our emotional well-being and overall outlook. It's essential to be mindful of their intentions, their level of empathy, and how they impact us. Selecting supportive, understanding, and positive people can provide comfort and encouragement, whereas those who are unsympathetic or critical may only add to our stress. Therefore, being careful about the company we keep during difficult periods can greatly affect how we cope and heal. Create some healthy boundaries around you so you will not be affected.

The least my family has done is to keep praying for me. It is often said that in challenging situations, one should surround themselves with supportive family and friends. I would advise distancing yourself from any relatives who remind you of your situation in a negative way. For the sake of your mental health and to feel better, it's important to avoid toxic people while you're waiting. I became good at avoiding communication with any relatives who were known for bringing up such conversations insensitively.

I don't like to be rude or disrespectful, so instead of potentially confronting them, I chose not to call or visit them. This way, there was no risk of a confrontation or walking out on them. I also avoided mentioning those relatives who, instead of offering words of love and encouragement, chose to focus on blame and accusations. When a woman is waiting to have a child, she is often emotionally vulnerable. During such times, what is needed most is genuine support and encouragement, not criticism for not visiting or calling.

Fortunately, I am blessed with a family that genuinely cares and supports me. We are a close-knit group, always checking in on each other, contributing to one another's well-being, and helping each other financially, emotionally and socially. We are not a family that neglects one another, and I feel incredibly fortunate to be part of such a loving and supportive Christian family.

Dealing With Years of Promotion Delay

One morning in February 2018, my mum expressed her frustration. Despite my dedication, hard work, and the accolades I received at work, I was yet to be promoted, not even once. She shared stories from her own banking career, recounting her struggles and victories. She mentioned that, in the past, promotions were given on a rotational basis and at specific intervals. It was puzzling to her that after spending eight years at the bank—where I was highly productive and a valuable team member—I had still not been promoted. It was particularly notable that people I had trained were being promoted while I remained in the same position. She asked me why and I said I do not know the reason.

A good friend Obioma once asked me if I had

ever been rude to anyone in the head office or if any of them had made unwelcome advances towards me. I assured him that I could not recall any such incidents. His concern was evident because he could not understand why I was being denied promotions despite my high level of productivity.

I had worked with about three different zonal managers, and one of them mentioned that my name had been put forward for the last promotion in 2017. He was surprised when my name was removed at the final stage.

This was also the case for a few of my friends who had spent seven to eight years at the bank without receiving a promotion.

As I returned to the office, it was nearing another year and another month of promotions. It was late March 2018, and the promotion lists, which are usually released every April, were approaching. To be honest, I wasn't looking forward to it. After seven long years and now entering my eighth year without a promotion, I had lost interest in the process. I wasn't excited or eager about the upcoming lists or the release dates.

Instead, I focused on doing what I knew best: managing funds, overseeing the vaults of the bank branch, handling the ATM terminals, and managing my cashiers. My expertise was in anything cash-related. I concentrated on being the best version of myself in my current role, striving to be the head of cash that others could rely on. Even though I was no longer a zonal officer, I continued to handle zonal reports efficiently. Each time a new zonal manager arrived, I was introduced to them as someone highly competent and reliable.

As April approached, people began speculating about whether the promotion lists would be released in the first or second week. I remained uninvolved in such conversations and, frankly, I wasn't interested.

Divine Protection

My friend Chioma used to drop me home after work because we live close to each other, and on that particular day, the 19th of April 2018, people were already becoming exhausted waiting for the promotion list. After we had finished for the day, we set off home, only to be involved in a serious car accident. A large truck collided with us, causing our vehicle to skid across the road. Miraculously, neither Chioma nor I sustained any broken bones or fractures. Chioma had some chest pain from the impact and the intense collision, but that was the extent of her injuries.

The glass in the section where I was sitting shattered, covering my entire body with glass fragments. I was speechless for a moment and could only utter, "Thank you, Jesus." I was overwhelmed by the thought of what could have happened. What if the story was about two young women who had just finished work and were killed in a car accident? Thankfully, we emerged with only bruises and no severe injuries. The glass did not penetrate any vital areas, such as my eyes.

We contacted our spouses, who came to pick us up from the scene. The vehicle was cleared away, and the driver who hit us was being questioned by the police. I wasn't interested in the details of the conversation; I was too shocked and kept thanking God for sparing our lives. When my husband arrived, he was astonished by the accident scene. It was indeed a miracle that we had no fractures, especially since Chioma's car was badly damaged.

We called our good friend Akin, who was shocked to hear about the incident. After leaving the scene, we moved the car to the branch, which was not far from the accident site. The accident had occurred just as we were reversing out of the office parking lot when the truck suddenly came from nowhere and collided with us.

My husband insisted I go to the hospital for a check-up, but I felt fine, as the seat belt had kept me securely in place and I had no significant impact injuries. The only discomfort I felt was from the vehicle's intense landing. After carefully removing all the glass fragments and taking a warm soapy bath, we treated the bruises with home remedies from our first aid kit. Though I was still a bit shaken and had some chest pain, I was reassured that no internal injuries were found in the X-ray the following day.

Promotion Comes from The Lord

The next day, 20th April, while I was at home in the evening, my phone started buzzing with calls and messages. I was a bit worried, wondering what was going on. As I opened the messages, one of them asked, "Have you seen the promotion list?" I replied, "Oh, is the promotion list out?" The response came back that it was out, and to my amazement, both my name and Chioma's name were on it. We had made the promotion list!

It was unbelievable. My first-ever promotion after eight years came just a day after I was involved in a near-fatal accident. It was a miracle that we were safe and that the promotion came through. Both Chioma and I were overjoyed and excited beyond measure.

The only thing I could say was, "God, you are indeed awesome." I truly felt that God had shown me His love after eight long years of waiting.

As I reflected on the events, I realised that my joy was not just about the promotion but about the affirmation of a deeper truth: waiting on God is never in vain. Each year of waiting, every moment of frustration and doubt, had not been wasted. Instead, they were part of a larger plan that unfolded with timing beyond my understanding.

The accident, which initially seemed like a tragic twist, turned into a testimony of grace and divine intervention. It highlighted the incredible contrast between the peril we faced and the unexpected blessing that followed.

In the midst of the celebration, I couldn't help but marvel at how God had shown His love and faithfulness in such a tangible way. This experience reinforced my belief that patience and faith are rewarded in ways we might not always expect, but always in accordance with a greater, perfect plan.

If you are seeking promotion, look to the Lord. The Bible assures us in Psalm 75:6-7 that promotion does not come from the east, west, or south; it comes from God alone. He is the ultimate judge who sets one up and brings another down according to His perfect wisdom and timing. Trust that God, who holds all authority, knows your heart, sees your efforts, and has a plan for your advancement. Continue to work diligently and faithfully, but let your trust be in Him. Your promotion is in His hands, and His timing is always perfect. Keep your faith strong, and believe that God will elevate you in due season.

As the chapter closed on this remarkable period of my life, I carried with me the assurance that waiting on God is never a waste of time. Even in the darkest moments, when the path seems uncertain, God's timing and blessings are perfect.

"I believe in being strong when everything seems to be going wrong. I believe that tomorrow is another day and I believe in Miracles"

—Audrey Hepburn

Chapter 8

Vacation

Working as Head Teller was a rewarding experience, and I was happy doing it effectively because I already had a good understanding of the role. It had been two years since my promotion, and ideally, with my performance so far, I should be on the 2021 promotion list, as I received my first promotion in 2018.

Enrolling in the Bank's Innovative Ideas Competition

While I was Head Teller, the bank launched a

competition focused on innovation. The winners would receive recognition, a commendation letter, and awards from the CEO of the bank. I registered for the contest, which involved answering questions, responding to prompts, and uploading documents to qualify.

Days passed, and I received an email informing me that I had been successful. We were selected from all the participants bank-wide and placed into groups of ten. My group specialised in small and medium enterprises (SMEs) and how to improve their operations. We developed an application that handled SME loans, queries, and networking opportunities for SME entrepreneurs, including access to free courses and training.

After two months of competition, my group emerged victorious. Out of ten groups, the first three were picked as winners, and my group was among them, securing second place. We received an award for innovation from the CEO. It was a fantastic moment in my banking career, as colleagues congratulated me from all directions.

This award also included a cash prize. It was a joyful period that helped me forget that I hadn't been promoted. The bankwide recognition from the bank was a great consolation.

My friends said, "Oh, Pamela, this is the time you will be promoted. On the next promotion list, you must be there. I can't see any way you will be denied a promotion after receiving a CEO award." I was confident that this time I would be promoted.

However, when the promotion list came out in April 2021, my name wasn't on it. This was a huge disappointment. I had never felt so devastated in my career. How could someone with a CEO award, commendation, and an impressive performance rating still be denied a promotion?

Invitation to a Vacation

My brother, Chiedu, who is the youngest in the family, is quite special. He lives in Dubai, thriving independently and doing well. Dubai has become my favourite vacation spot, thanks to him. After hearing the news of my promotion denials in the

April 2021 promotion list, he was devastated. He then invited me to Dubai for a vacation to rest and recuperate.

I told him, "This is just post-pandemic and people are still dealing with the aftermath. Travelling to Dubai for a vacation will be quite challenging." But he said, "We'll work it out."

I have a very supportive husband. Whenever it comes to anything that can give me peace of mind or joy, he always supports it, even if it means denying himself comfort. So, I told him I wanted to go to Dubai for a holiday. He suggested I plan a solo trip to Dubai to get some fresh air after everything that had happened.

At that time, travelling to Dubai from Nigeria was difficult due to issues between Nigeria and Emirates. The only option available was travelling from Benin Republic. I started making inquiries and found out the best way to travel to Dubai via Cotonou. It was quite expensive, involving getting to and crossing the border, plus all the required Coronavirus tests in Benin Republic.

I knew there was no issue with me having the virus, as we had been tested in the office and were clear. My flight and hotel were booked. My friend and colleague, Tom, who is from Badagry—a border town close to Cotonou—had his brother help me cross the border and check into the hotel. My flight was scheduled for three days later, so I paid for two nights in the hotel.

The COVID-19 centre was busy, mostly with Nigerians wanting to travel for a break or business. Nigerians love a good holiday, no matter the cost. I waited patiently for my turn, took my COVID-19 test, and was told to come back the next day for the results. We could also check the results online.

Obstacles in My Way

That evening, the agent visited my hotel room. We tried checking my results online, but they were not yet uploaded. Late at night, he was finally able to access them. The results showed that I was positive. It was the most devastating news I'd ever received. This meant I couldn't fly. I couldn't wrap my head around it. Why was this happening? I just wanted to go on holiday to clear my head, see my younger brother, and relax.

The next morning, I went to the COVID-19 centre and was told I couldn't fly and needed treatment. I was advised to come back in 14 days. I had to return to Nigeria, cancel my flight, and reschedule it for 16 to 17 days later, hoping I would be cleared by then.

After spending so much money and stress passing the border again, I travelled back to Nigeria. Thankfully, my friend's brother, David helped me get to Badagry, where I rested for the night before heading to Nigeria the next morning. I already told my husband what had happened, so he was expecting me. We prayed over the phone, and he reassured me that this infectious disease is not a death sentence.

At that point, I wasn't worried about my health because I had no symptoms. My main concern was the stress of not being able to travel. Why was I in a situation where I had to endure such stress?

In times like these, it feels as if the whole world

is against you. But I want to encourage you: this is the time to hold on to the people you love and your beliefs.

My knowledge of the scriptures and the Word of God kept me grounded during this challenging time. Facing a denied promotion, extra stress, and the added burden of expensive COVID-19 tests and treatment was a lot to handle. Testing positive and needing to return to Nigeria to come back in 14-15 days was unimaginable.

I wasn't worried about whether I would recover or not because I had assurance that I would be fine as this is just a setback. At this point, I pray and empathise with families who have lost loved ones to this deadly virus. I send my sincere condolences to the frontline staff who fought the fight for survival while taking care of those who were sick due to the virus. You are indeed heroes.

When I got back home, I told my husband to stay away to avoid contracting COVID-19, but he laughed it off. As a man of faith, he was confident he wouldn't be affected. Before getting to Asaba, I stopped briefly at my younger brother Chuks's house in Benin Republic. He and his wife, Jennifer, welcomed me warmly. Family is truly invaluable. They showed no signs of avoiding me, even though I kept reminding them to maintain their distance.

I stayed with them for 24 hours, during which Jennifer prepared local herbs believed to be effective against the virus. Although my brother wanted me to stay longer, I left the next day to start treatment.

Returning home, my husband's reception was as warm as ever; he made no effort to avoid me. I began my treatment, which was expensive but necessary. My parents also called frequently to check on me.

Though many people reported symptoms of COVID-19, I experienced no loss of appetite or significant symptoms, only a mild fever. After seven to eight days of treatment, I returned to the clinic in Nigeria for a test. Mrs Tobi, who works at the hospital and is like a mother to the family, advised me to wait until the 10th day before testing again.

Despite my anxiety, I followed her advice.

When I completed my medication and tested again, the results were negative. On the 11th day, I started my journey back to Lagos. I arrived in the Benin Republic on the 13th day, as the doctor had suggested I return on the 14th day for a follow-up test to confirm my recovery.

I arrived at the Testing Centre and registered for another test. After the test was completed, I returned to my hotel room and waited anxiously for the results to be uploaded online, but they never appeared. On the 15th day, I went back to the COVID-19 Centre in the Benin Republic, where I met with a new doctor. To my surprise, he asked me to register for another test, despite being told by a previous doctor that I would be eligible for testing on the 14th day, which I had done.

The new doctor claimed I was supposed to remain at the COVID-19 Centre and not leave. I explained that I had not been informed of this and detailed the treatment I had received. The doctor insisted that I should have taken medication from the COVID-19 Centre, which was new information to me. When he switched to speaking French, I had to inform him that I could not understand the language. His manner was both rude and unhelpful. He stated that I would not be able to travel and advised me to return in two days.

I was devastated, especially as I had a flight booked for the 16th day and was unwilling to cancel it again. The doctor's refusal seemed unjustifiable, and I left his consulting room in tears. At the reception of the COVID-19 Centre, I bowed my head and prayed, asking God if He had abandoned me. I was desperate to travel and could not bear the thought of booking another flight or cancelling it once more.

I called my younger brother, who was also heartbroken. I asked him not to worry but to be hopeful and see what happens next. I felt quite lost at that moment.

Divine Helper

A young man who happened to be a member of staff at the testing centre approached me. He recognised me from my previous visits and asked why I was still there. I explained my situation with the doctor. He was puzzled by the doctor's insistence on a return visit and suggested I check if my results were available online. I told him they had not been uploaded.

The young man took my registration number and asked me to wait. After about 20 minutes, he returned and told me to check the website again. To my amazement, my results were now uploaded as negative. He was puzzled as well, questioning why the doctor hadn't updated the results and why I was being asked to return in two days when my results were clearly negative.

I asked the young man the charge for the services he had rendered, but he refused any payment. I was astonished and felt like this was a divine intervention. It was as if my prayers had been answered in an unexpected way. Was he an angel assigned by God to help me? He definitely was one because this is a rare gesture.

The young man assured me that my results were authentic and would be accepted at the airport. He even gave me his contact number in case I faced any issues. With his reassurance, I felt a renewed sense of hope and relief. I just couldn't believe it and hesitated to leave. He kept reassuring me that everything was alright. I returned to my hotel, overwhelmed with gratitude, and thanked God for this unexpected turn of events.

I called my husband to share the good news, and he was as shocked as I was. I checked the results again, and they were still online. I called my younger brother, and he was so excited because he had checked online and hadn't found any close date to reschedule if I needed to, so I didn't need to cancel.

Your Divine Helper is Coming

When you are walking in the divine will of God, He will always send divine helpers to your assistance. A divine helper is someone specifically assigned by God to help you fulfil your assignment or achieve a goal. This young man was such a helper to me.

If we look at the Bible, there are numerous examples of divine helpers appearing in times of need. One notable instance is the story of Joseph. While imprisoned in Egypt, Joseph interprets the dreams of Pharaoh's cupbearer and baker. The cupbearer once restored to his position, eventually remembers Joseph and mentions him to Pharaoh when Pharaoh has troubling dreams. Joseph's interpretation of Pharaoh's dreams leads to his rise to power as the governor of Egypt, ultimately saving many people from famine. The cupbearer was a divine helper.

This example, among many others, shows how God orchestrates divine assistance at crucial moments. It is important to keep your eyes and heart open, as God is sending a divine helper into your life to support you in accomplishing what He has called you to do. Be attentive and receptive to these helpers, for they are instrumental in fulfilling God's purpose for your life.

Arrival in Dubai

The following day, I arrived at the airport, and the clearance process went smoothly. I boarded my flight to Dubai and when I arrived, my younger brother, was waiting for me at the airport and he was overjoyed.

In Dubai, everything went smoothly. My brother helped me settle in, though I soon developed a high fever. We speculated that it might be stress or lack of rest, but being in Dubai was exactly what I needed at the time. After a short rest, I felt better, and we went shopping for ingredients to make Jollof rice, which my younger brother had been eagerly anticipating. I unpacked and got my brother some Indomie, a special kind of noodles different from those available in Dubai. I also brought him some local foodstuffs for soup that were unavailable in Dubai.

The Dubai trip was wonderful. We enjoyed

local delights, had a desert ride, visited Starbucks, and explored many other pleasant places in Dubai. It was one of the best holidays I've had. My brother did everything possible to help me relax and enjoy the vacation, making it a fantastic experience.

As I returned to Nigeria, I reflected on how valuable it is to take breaks, travel, and experience new environments. Such trips are not only refreshing but also beneficial for mental health.

"We travel not to escape life
but for life not to escape us."

— Unknown

A Few Pictures From My Dubai Vacation with Chiedu

Chapter 9

Revisit

After the ectopic pregnancy, I deliberately avoided seeing any doctors. It was a conscious decision to stay away from reminders of my past ordeal. Nearly a decade had passed without a single visit to a clinic, and despite the hopeful longing for pregnancy, nothing changed.

Friends, both from church and beyond, frequently asked if I had tried various treatments. Their well-meaning suggestions included several medical interventions, but I avoided them all. Even my husband respected my decision, believing that this was a personal journey I needed to come to terms with.

I often told myself that if it was meant to be, it would happen. Yet, I also acknowledged that medical professionals possess valuable skills and knowledge that could potentially assist us. Sometimes, a check-up is necessary to understand what is happening within our bodies. As the years passed, I realised that while I wasn't getting any younger, I had focused solely on my job which offered neither the distraction nor the fulfilment I needed.

Instead, I found solace and joy in my faith, my family, and close friends. My Bible provided spiritual comfort, and my loved ones offered unwavering support. I built strong relationships both at work and in my personal life. Even though many of my friends were scattered across various branches in Nigeria, their support was steadfast. These were friends who listened, comforted, and understood me, making it clear how crucial it is to cultivate such relationships.

Building these connections is not merely about

receiving; it's about giving generously and sincerely. While we might not always get back what we put in, the act of kindness itself is a reflection of our values. Just as God gave His Son for our salvation, we too should strive to be good to others, consciously and deliberately.

I take pride in knowing that today, I can reach out to any of those friends, no matter the time or place, and they will be there to help me as I was for them during their own struggles. This mutual support and understanding highlight the true essence of compassion and friendship.

One morning, my friend Obioma called me from one of the branches and suggested I see a doctor, especially since everyone around me was recommending it. I agreed, as my husband and I had already planned to see a doctor that weekend. This was based on a recommendation from a deacon at my church, who encouraged me to seek medical advice. It felt like the reassurance I needed.

After nearly nine years since my ectopic pregnancy experience, I was finally revisiting issues related to reproduction. We visited a renowned gynaecologist known for his extensive experience in the field. The doctor recommended several tests, which we promptly underwent. The following day, when we returned to pick up the results, he suggested considering other medical procedures. However, before making a final recommendation, he wanted to assess the condition of my remaining fallopian tube, given that I had lost one during the ectopic pregnancy.

He referred me for an HSG procedure, which I had heard about from my sister-in-law. She had described it as an excruciatingly painful experience, which is why I had been avoiding gynaecologists and any potential pain. Despite my fears, I knew I had to go through with it.

Hospital Visit

On the appointed day, my husband accompanied me to the hospital. He stayed by my side through the registration and vital checks for the HSG. HSG stands for Hysterosalpingography. It is a radiologic procedure used to examine a woman's reproductive organs, specifically the uterus and fallopian tubes. When it was finally my turn, I went into the room, and the doctor encouraged me to relax as the procedure began.

From the start, I was in agony, crying and screaming. My husband, waiting outside the door, could hear my distress and was visibly uncomfortable. The initial attempt lasted about 20 minutes, but the doctor struggled to get a clear image of my tube because my crying caused disruptions. Consequently, we had to repeat the procedure. During the break, my husband came in to comfort me, offering reassurance and prayers.

The second attempt was intensely painful. I began to vomit uncontrollably, with my husband trying to help and manage the situation. Despite our efforts, the process left me feeling extremely weak and in significant pain. The doctor concluded the procedure and explained that the pain would eventually subside and advised me to rest and avoid eating immediately.

Once we got home, I continued to vomit for

over ten hours, unable to keep anything down. The food my husband managed to get for me was untouched, and I could barely drink a bottle of Sprite. I felt completely drained, both physically and emotionally, struggling with the persistent nausea and weakness.

The vomiting persisted for over ten hours, continuing intermittently throughout the night. I lost all sense of strength, and my sense of smell disappeared. I felt terribly weak.

I swore I would never undergo this procedure again, even if it were the only option for having a baby. I vowed to myself never to endure this pain again. I marvelled at what women go through and the challenges working women face. I was expected to be back in the office in two days' time.

By the next day, I felt a bit better and managed to eat a small amount of food, although the pain persisted. My husband called the specialist who performed the HSG procedure to ask if it was normal to still be in pain and vomiting after 24 hours. The specialist was surprised by the vomiting but said that extended pain could be normal for some people. Fortunately, the vomiting stopped the following afternoon, and I began to regain my strength gradually. The thought of returning to work was daunting, but as a working professional, showing up is part of the job.

We live in a country where people envy the kind of job I have. Employers are often eager to find someone else who can do the job for less. I had to brace myself because my position was sensitive, being the Head of Cash. This role required experience, trust, dedication, and years of service. It wasn't a position that could be contracted out, so I was relatively secure. However, it also demanded my constant presence, except for leave days.

Finding someone to fill in for me during my absence was often a hassle, especially when the only available relief officer might be in another location. So, despite my pain, weakness, and worries, I had to perform my duties.

When we revisited the doctor with the results over the weekend, he conducted a comprehensive review of the X-rays and internal organ scans. He recommended various medical procedures, given that my only tube was still intact. He advised against putting additional strain on the existing tube and suggested other procedures.

We thanked him for his advice. The alternative medical procedures were something my husband and I had never seriously considered. While we were not opposed to them, we felt it was not yet the time for us to pursue them. We decided to hold on to our faith, continue praying, and trust in God until we felt convinced to go ahead with these procedures.

> *"Tomorrow when I awake, the slate will be clean and a new day will stretch before me."*
>
> **— Lori Hatcher**

Chapter 10

Still Waiting, Still Hopeful

Psalm 27:14

"Wait on the Lord: be of good courage, and he shall strengthen thine heart: wait, I say, on the Lord."

Isaiah 40:31

"But they that wait upon the Lord shall renew their strength; they shall mount up with wings as eagles; they shall run, and not be weary; and they shall walk, and not faint."

Isaiah 64:4

"For since the beginning of the world men have not heard, nor perceived by the ear, neither hath the eye seen, O God, beside thee, what he hath prepared for him that waiteth for him."

These are strong scriptures that encourage me to keep waiting and remain hopeful. God will always honour His Word. The God who honours the institution of marriage and who created women also understands that when a woman gets married, one of her major desires—particularly in the part of the world where I come from—is to have a child. While some may not share this desire, I know that the majority of women do.

I am speaking to those who are waiting and believing in God for something. I have not given up, and neither should you. Waiting on God is always the best course of action. There will always be guidance on what to do or what to eat. The essence is believing and trusting that what God says will come to pass, that He will do what He has promised, and that He will answer our earnest prayers.

I trust in the Lord with all my heart and lean not on my own understanding. I know that my God, whom I have waited for, will answer. To all the working women balancing office duties, dealing with the loss of a child, undergoing surgery, and striving to be a good wife and mother—this is a reminder that God has made us versatile.

Women are multi-talented and great multitaskers. We have been blessed to handle and endure many responsibilities. A woman can go to work, return home, cook, care for the children, wash clothes, look after her husband, and continue this routine daily. Do not withdraw from your responsibilities just because you have experienced pain. I encourage you to hold on to your faith.

"*Ada Úkwú*," is that great daughter, one who will maintain a strong connection with her home, family, and colleagues, and build valuable relationships. Over the years, I have cultivated a network of trusted friends who I can call upon at any time. I strive to remain loving, caring, and kind. I have not allowed my personal pain or circumstances to affect my relationships with people, including my siblings and parents. I have learned that challenges are part of life, but overcoming them makes me a champion.

Pain will always be present. How we navigate through it is what truly matters. How we overcome these challenges is key. For me, it involves holding on to the Word of God, maintaining strong bonds with family, nurturing enduring friendships, and having a very loving spouse.

Single Lady, Wait

I must emphasise the importance of marrying a friend. Do not rush into marriage as a young woman, and do not feel pressured to marry. In Africa, there is often pressure on women approaching their 30s and 40s to settle down. This pressure can sometimes lead people to make poor choices. Women may find themselves with the wrong partner, or men may end up with the wrong woman.

The key word here is "wait." While you are waiting, watch and pray. Observe the people around you and ask God to open your eyes to see clearly. Seek God's guidance in directing you. Prayer is an essential part of this process.

You need to pray and wait for God to guide you to your spouse. I didn't marry early, but I am grateful to God that I married my friend. Despite not having children, I am happy in my marriage. My husband loves me deeply; he supports me in going on vacation if I wish and is always there for me. He dotes on me because I wasn't in a rush or looking to marry a billionaire. Sincerely, I feel richer than the wealthiest wife because I have the best husband, parents, siblings, and friends. Waiting on God means waiting in every aspect of life.

Whether you are waiting for a job as a young woman, do not succumb to the pressure of compromising your values to get one. I've heard many young women say that you can't get a job unless you compromise yourself or sleep with someone. That is not true. I secured my job without doing that, and I know many women who have found employment by waiting patiently and focusing on self-development.

Don't think that after years of waiting for a spouse, you are entitled to misbehave because you can't have children. That's not the case. You should continue to wait on the Lord, believe, and strive to be the best version of yourself. This is not the time to party away your sorrows or fall into depression because of a loss. It's painful, and I understand the depth of that pain—I've been there. If it means seeking therapy or changing your environment for better mental health, please do so.

Above all, my scripture is my medicine. The Word of God is my remedy and has kept me sane in a world filled with pain. Waiting on God has been incredibly helpful to me. As I mentioned, I received my first promotion after eight years. Even without those promotions, I never lacked. God has always been there for me and will always be there for us.

I want to encourage you, if you are feeling overwhelmed, to keep waiting. Keep believing and trusting God, whether you are still waiting for a spouse or facing other challenges. Trust in the Lord. Though the vision may tarry, it will surely come and not delay. So, let us be patient, keep ourselves happy, and maintain our health and well-being.

Go on vacations, visit your loved ones, and keep sowing your seeds of love. Do not cut yourself off from the world, even if it feels like the world has turned its back on you. Continue to act with kindness and love.

One of my extracurricular activities was being a member of the Rotary Club. I was fortunate to rise to the position of Rotaract Club President during my university days in the 2002-2003 Rotary year, which had the theme "Sow the Seeds of Love." This experience has stayed with me, and I strive to sow seeds of love wherever I go. While I may not be perfect, I am constantly trying to improve, and I hope to be better every day.

I encourage you to find activities that bring you joy. Engage in something positive, whether it's exercise, learning a new skill, seeing a movie, watching football (my Chelsea), or joining a club like Rotaract, which focuses on helping the less privileged. There are many positive activities that can help keep you sane. In church, there are weekly activities you can get involved in, such as the choir, decoration, cleaning, and welfare. Join one of these groups to keep yourself occupied and prevent idleness. Remember, an idle mind is the devil's playground, which can lead to negativity and potentially to depression.

I encourage you to read the scriptures, attend good gatherings, participate in church programmes, and involve yourself in activities that keep you happy. God will honour His Word in your life. Also, remember to put your faith into action. You cannot claim to have faith without actively believing and trusting that God will bless you. As I have said, I am still waiting and hopeful, and the story of "ADA ÚKWÚ" is still being written.

"For the vision is yet for an appointed time,
but at the end it shall speak, and not lie:
though it tarry, wait for it; because it
will surely come, it will not tarry."

— Habakkuk 2:3

Printed in Great Britain
by Amazon

49915298R00079